YOU MUST REMEMBER THIS

1951

MILESTONES, MEMORIES,
TRIVIA AND FACTS, NEWS EVENTS,
PROMINENT PERSONALITIES &
SPORTS HIGHLIGHTS OF THE YEAR

TO :

FROM :

MESSAGE :

selected and researched
by
mary a. pradt

WARNER TREASURES™

PUBLISHED BY WARNER BOOKS

A TIME WARNER COMPANY

Warner Books, Inc.
1271 Avenue of the Americas
New York, New York 10020

Warner Treasures is a
trademark of Warner Books, Inc.

A Time Warner Company

DESIGN:
CAROL BOKUNIEWICZ DESIGN
PRINTED IN SINGAPORE
FIRST PRINTING : MAY 1995
10 9 8 7 6 5 4 3 2 1
ISBN : 0-446-91026-0

The U.S. tested atomic weapons in Nevada, and in May the U.S. acknowledged its testing of the hydrogen bomb in the mid-Pacific near Eniwetok. The H-bomb would be hundreds of times more powerful than the bombs used on Hiroshima and Nagasaki.

Anti-Communist fervor heated up considerably in 1951. At the end of March, husband and wife Julius and Ethel Rosenberg were found guilty of wartime espionage and were convicted of passing American A-bomb secrets to the Soviets. In April they were sentenced to death.

newsreel

IN JANUARY, WASHINGTON FROZE PRICES AND WAGES, IN ORDER TO CURB INFLATION. AMERICAN PER CAPITA ANNUAL INCOME WAS $1,436, UP 9 PERCENT IN ONE YEAR, AND THE HIGHEST TOTAL IN HISTORY. AVERAGE INCOMES RANGED FROM $698 IN MISSISSIPPI TO $1,986 IN WASHINGTON, D.C.

President Truman fired **Douglas MacArthur**, who was leading the Korean War effort, for challenging the president's foreign policy. On April 20, the fired general received a triumphal welcome in a New York ticker-tape parade.

THE KOREAN WAR DOMINATED THE NEWS ALL YEAR.

IN IRAN, THE OIL INDUSTRY WAS NATIONALIZED AND BRITISH OIL INSTALLATIONS WERE SEIZED.

headlines international

General Matthew Ridgway replaced MacArthur in the Far Eastern command. The Soviets pressed for a cease-fire. By the end of November, UN and Communist negotiators reached agreement on a truce plan for Korea, basically dividing the country along the 38th Parallel. By Christmas, the Korean Communists had released a list of the more than 3,000 Allied prisoners of war they were holding.

A contrite West German parliament voted in September to make reparations to Jews for the money stolen from them during the war—estimated as high as $600 million. East Germany did not make any admissions of guilt or agree to pay reparations.

Libya attained independence December 24. The former Italian colony ranked as the poorest country in the world and was the first organized under UN auspices.

In May, Tibet submitted to Communist China officially, as the Dalai Lama, 16, signed an agreement with the Peking government.

The King and I, a Rodgers and Hammerstein musical, opened on Broadway March 29, with Gertrude Lawrence and Yul Brynner starring. It was based on the true story of a British teacher who taught the 67 children of the King of Siam at the time of the American Civil War.

Margaret Truman, 26, the president's daughter and a professional singer, made her radio acting debut on NBC's "Jackpot." Jimmy Stewart co-starred, and stuttered more than usual in the April broadcast.

cultural
milestones

TELEVISION WAS TRANSFORMING THE SOCIETY TO A DEGREE NOT SEEN SINCE THE DAWN OF THE AUTOMOBILE, ACCORDING TO A STUDY IN THE *NEW YORK TIMES*. TV WAS AFFECTING EVERYTHING FROM POLITICS TO LEISURE TIME, HOW MUCH PEOPLE READ, AND HOW CHILDREN WERE BROUGHT UP.

The American Telephone and Telegraph Company announced in May that it had one million shareholders, a first in U.S. business history.

Ricky Ricardo UNFAIR

television

In May, the Radio Corporation of America broadcast color TV programs from the Empire State Building. Unlike a competing CBS system, the signal could be received by black-and-white sets. Good thing, too, because there were only about 30 sets in the New York area that could get the color signal.

Television had penetrated almost one quarter of American households; there were 10.3 million TV households, or 23.5%. A total of 107 TV stations were operating in 63 cities, within range of 62 percent of the American population. The FCC predicted in November that the U.S. would have 1,200 to 1,500 TV stations within five years.

Princess Elizabeth of Britain and her husband, the Duke of Edinburgh, visited Windsor, Ontario, in October and made their debut in the first international telecast—NBC's Detroit station carried this milestone.

TOP-RATED TV SERIES FALL 1951 SEASON

1. "Arthur Godfrey's Talent Scouts" (CBS)

2. "Texaco Star Theater" (NBC)

3. "I Love Lucy" (CBS)

4. "The Red Skelton Show" (NBC)

5. "The Colgate Comedy Hour" (NBC)

6. "Arthur Godfrey and His Friends" (CBS)

7. "Fireside Theater" (NBC)

8. "Your Show of Shows" (NBC)

9. "The Jack Benny Show" (CBS)

10. "You Bet Your Life" (NBC)

11. "Mama" (CBS)

12. "Philco TV Playhouse" (NBC)

13. "Amos 'n' Andy" (CBS)

14. "Gangbusters" (NBC)

15. "Big Town" (CBS)

milestones

celeb wedding of the year

Reza Pahlevi, the Shah of Iran, 31, married Soraya Esfandiari, 19, the

daughter of a rebel chieftain, in a Muslim ceremony in February. More

than 2,000 guests attended the festivities at the Gulistan Palace in Tehran.

celeb births

CRYSTAL GAYLE, country western singer, was born January 9.

CHARO, ebullient performer, was born Maria Martinez January 15, in Murcia, Spain.

MEL GIBSON, actor, was born January 3.

YAKOV SMIRNOFF, comedian, was born January 24 in Odessa.

ED MARINARO, actor, was born March 31.

OLIVIA HUSSEY, actress, was born in Buenos Aires April 17.

TONY DANZA, actor and comedian, was born in Brooklyn April 21.

HELEN SHAVER, actress, was born in Ontario, Canada, February 24.

ANJELICA HUSTON, actress and daughter of the famous director/actor John Huston, was born July 8.

KURT RUSSELL, actor, was born March 17.

JANE SEYMOUR, actress, was born February 15.

EDWARD "TOO TALL" JONES, former boxer and football star, was born February 23.

PAT BRADLEY, a standard-setting LPGA golfer, first woman to win the sport's four-tournament Grand Slam, was born March 24.

DAVE WINFIELD, baseball player, was born October 3.

ANATOLI KARPOV, Soviet chess whiz, was born May 23.

SALLY K. RIDE, the first American woman in space, was born May 26.

MICHAEL KEATON, hugely popular actor and director, was born September 9.

HARRY HAMLIN, actor, was born October 31.

STING, rock star, was born October 2.

HELOISE CRUSE EVANS, the newspaper columnist and dispenser of household hints, was born April 15.

DEATHS

Charles Nessler, inventor of the permanent wave and false eyelashes, died January 22 at 78.

Ferdinand Porsche, the German engineer who designed the Volkswagen Beetle, one of the world's most successful cars, died in Stuttgart January 18. He was 75.

Fanny Brice, the original Broadway Funny Girl, died at 59 on May 29.

Arnold Schoenberg, composer and inventor of the twelve-tone system, died July 13.

William Randolph Hearst, flamboyant newspaper tycoon, who lived with a mistress, Marion Davies, for 30 years (while still married to his wife), died August 14 at the age of 88.

Will K. Kellogg, breakfast-cereal entrepreneur, passed away October 6 at the age of 91.

Harold Ross, editor and founder of *The New Yorker*, passed away at 59 in December.

Sinclair Lewis, Pulitzer and Nobel-winning author, passed on at 65 in Rome in January.

André Gide, French novelist, succumbed to pneumonia at 81 in February.

1. **because of you** was the first million-selling hit for Tony Bennett. It was on the top of the Hit Parade for 11 weeks in 1951 and was the #1 hit of the year.

2. **the tennessee waltz** released by Patti Page in 1950, was the #2 hit of the year. In 1965, Tennessee chose it as the official state song.

3. **too young** introduced by Johnny Desmond, was also recorded by Nat "King" Cole, whose performance took it to the top of the charts, where it lodged for a dozen weeks.

4. **how high the moon** was a million-selling disk for Les Paul and Mary Ford.

5. **cold, cold heart** written by Hank Williams and recorded by him, became Williams's seventh million-seller. Tony Bennett's version also sold a million.

hit music

HANK WILLIAMS

6. **down yonder** introduced in New Orleans in 1921, was a hit in 1951 for country pianist Del Wood.

7. **be my love** as recorded by Mario Lanza, was introduced in the 1950 movie musical *Toast of New Orleans*. The melody is dramatic and shows a tenor's vocal range and power.

7. **come on-a my house** was recorded by Rosemary Clooney, at the urging of Mitch Miller. It became Clooney's first gold record.

8. **my heart cries for you** composed by Percy Faith, was recorded by Guy Mitchell.

TONY BENNETT

Another novelty song from a movie musical, *Royal Wedding*, was introduced by Fred Astaire and Jane Powell; it was titled "How Could You Believe Me When I Said I Loved You When You Know I've Been a Liar All My Life?" It's sometimes called just "The Liar Song."

"The Aba Daba Honeymoon," an oldie from 1914, was revived in the movie *Two Weeks with Love*, and made a hit by Debbie Reynolds and Carleton Carpenter on the soundtrack. This nonsense song about a monkey honeymoon sold 3 million copies.

"MOCKIN' BIRD HILL," RECORDED BY LES PAUL AND MARY FORD, WAS THE FIRST TRUE MULTITRACK RECORDING.

fiction

1. **from here to eternity**
   by james jones

2. **the caine mutiny**
   by herman wouk

3. **moses**
   by sholem asch

4. **the cardinal**
   by henry morton robinson

5. **a woman
   called fancy**
   by frank yerby

6. **the cruel sea**
   by nicholas monsarrat

7. **melville goodwin,
   u.s.a.**
   by john marquand

8. **return to paradise**
   by james michener

9. **the foundling**
   by cardinal spellman

10. **the wanderer**
    by mika waltari

J. D. Salinger's first novel, **The Catcher in the Rye,** was published and became an instant success with teens and college students. It retains its cult following to this day.

bestselling

14

books

1. **look younger, live longer**
   by gaylord hauser
2. **betty crocker's picture cookbook**
3. **washington confidential**
   by jack lait and lee mortimer
4. **better homes and gardens garden book**
5. **better homes and gardens handyman's book**
6. **the sea around us**
   by rachel carson
7. **thorndike barnhart comprehensive desk dictionary**
   ed. by clarence l. barnhart
8. **pogo**
   cartoon book by walt kelly
9. **kon-tiki**
   by thor heyerdahl
10. *the new yorker* **twenty-fifth anniversary album**

BOXING

It was an eventful year in sports. **Sugar Ray Robinson**, for five years the welter-weight king, February 14 KO'd Jake LaMotta for the middleweight crown. In July, Brit Randy Turpin beat Sugar Ray in the most stunning upset in 25 years' boxing history. For Robinson, it was only his second loss in 133 bouts. In September, Sugar Ray defeated Turpin and brought the world middleweight crown back to the U.S. **"Kid" Gavilan** took the world welterweight title from **Johnny Bratton**. In June, Joe Louis KO'd Lee Savold in a comeback bout. In October, Rocky Marciano, 27, stopped Joe Louis's bid to become the first to regain a heavyweight title.

It was a momentous **year in baseball.**
Joe DiMaggio, "the Yankee Clipper," signed his
third $100,000 contract in a row. The New York Giants
took the pennant on Bobby Thompson's "shot heard
'round the world," a ninth-inning homer. Then the
Yankees triumphed over the Giants in an all-New York
World Series, 4–3 in the sixth game.

WIMBLEDON CHAIRMAN SIR LOUIS GRIEG
STATED HE WISHED TO SEE NO MORE "BIKI-
NI BATHING DRESSES" AT THE MATCHES.

sports

TOUR DE FRANCE IN JULY.

SWISS RACER HUGO KOBLET WON THE

BELANGER SPECIAL, AVERAGING 126 MPH.

LEE WALLARD WON THE INDY 500 IN A

**In the Rose Bowl
in Pasadena,
Michigan blanked
California 14–0.
On December 23,
the L.A. Rams
downed the
Cleveland Browns
24–17, for the
pro title.**

At Wimbledon, Dick Savitt
bested Ken McGregor 6–4,
6–4, 6-4. Dorothy Hart won
over Shirley Fry, 6–1, 6–0.
Maureen Connolly, 16, became
the youngest woman to win the
title in the **U.S. Tennis
Championships** at Forest
Hills in September. "Little Mo"
defeated veteran Shirley Fry.

An American in Paris was a big winner. It took Best Picture, writing, color cinematography, and art direction/set decoration and color costume design honors. **Humphrey Bogart** scored as Best Actor for his role in *The African Queen* opposite Katharine Hepburn. **Vivian Leigh** took Best Actress Oscar, winning for her role in *Streetcar*. **Karl Malden** took Supporting Actor and **Kim Hunter** Supporting Actress Oscars for their roles in *Streetcar*. **George Stevens** won the Best Director Oscar for *A Place in the Sun*, which also took black-and-white cinematography and scoring honors. **Edith Head**'s costumes for the film were also awarded an Oscar.

There were numerous war movies, most of them dealing with World War II, and only a few documentaries dealing with the Korean conflict. The best war film of the year, directed by John Huston, was **The Red Badge of Courage**, based on Stephen Crane's Civil War novel. **The Desert Fox,** portraying the life of Field Marshal Rommel, encountered some censorship because it seemed to show the Nazi as a hero.

There were 23,120 movie theaters in the U.S., of which 3,323 were drive-ins.

Hollywood began to defend itself in 1951; its "Movietime U.S.A." industry campaign was designed to focus on the quality of new films and the positive values of movies of the past. It was a $1 million campaign, and many Hollywood personalities traveled around the country to promote the industry's image.

Among the more notable of the 400 films released during the year were: *A Place in the Sun, A Streetcar Named Desire, Born Yesterday, Death of a Salesman,* and *Detective Story. An American in Paris* led the long list of musicals.

movies

'51 cars

One sweet convertible was the Jaguar-esque Cunningham Model C-1. General Motors, of course, would suggest the "jet-back" look of a Buick Riviera, with its aerodynamic lines and speedy-looking chrome strips from front to back fender.

Or, for the two-car family, an Estate Wagon, with Dynaflow Drive (automatic transmission) available if you wished it: a good idea if "the Little Woman" would be driving.

Climax of a season when texture is paramount: Kurli Flur, the fabric that comes honestly by its fur look, its finger-deep fur feel. Altogether wonderful new fusion of real fur and finest wool, for your most important coat: the far-flung, velvet paved greatcoat. Available with Milium linings. Colors: Solid beige or grey. Cross Dyed: Black with White, Navy with White, Red, Gold, Green, Blue and Spice with Black. About $100 at fine stores. Write Baitch & Castaldi, 230 W. 39th St., N. Y. for one nearest you.

KURLI FLUR

the fur-look fabric
made with fur

luxury-licensed by
LIMIGER

BAITCH & CASTALDI

Fabric dominated all phases of fashion, more significant than color or silhouette. Fabrics were stiff, textured, often three-dimensional. Poodle cloth, a woolen fabric as furry and thick as the real thing, appeared in innumerable versions and gave new importance to the winter coat.

At this time the designers' dicta, especially the French, decreed the all-important hem length. Measurements were still given from the floor, even though heel heights would vary. Hems, according to **Dior** in 1951, should be 14"; he did try some suits with skirts 13" from the floor.

Small hats, smooth hairdos, lower-heeled, pointier-toed footwear, small cinched waistlines, smooth-fitting and hip-covering bodices, and large, flat handbags were in. Large, jangly jewelry completed the look.

Black came into its own as a color for fall.

fashion

Aside from the high-fashion trends, as families started watching more television, going out less, and entertaining at home more, loungewear or at-home wear came into its own, both for men and women. Slippers, hostess gowns, and lounging jackets opened up a whole new category of fashion for manufacturers to exploit.

final
factoid

In December, a **bagel shortage** loomed in New York, due to a labor dispute. On an average weekend, New Yorkers consumed 1.2 million bagels. Lox sales were down 30 to 50 percent.

archive photos: pages 1, 10, 15, 20, 21, inside back cover.

associated press: pages 5, 16,

photofest: inside front cover, pages 3, 6, 8, 9, 12, 13, 17, 18, 19.

original photography:
beth phillips: pages 14, 22, 25.

book cover:
courtesy of jessy randell and glenn horowitz; page 14

photo research:
alice albert

coordination:
rustyn birch

design:
carol bokuniewicz design
paul ritter

'51